ESSENTIAL LIFE HACKS FOR KIDS AGE 6

BY TAYLOR FINN

Join our mailing list to be notified of new products!

Copyright © 2022 by Scholastic Arte Press
All rights reserved. This book or any portion thereof
may not be reproduced or used in any manner whatsoever
without the express written permission of the publisher
except for the use of brief quotations in a book review.
Printed in the United States of America
First Printing, 2022
Scholastic Arte Press
www.scholasticartepress.com

Table Of Contents

01 Super Dresser Explorer

02 Manners Magic: The Power of Politeness

03 Sharing Stars

04 Street Safety Safari

05 Stranger Safety Squad

06 911 Explorers

07 Coin Counting Quest

08 Table Setting Wizards

09 Litter-Free Wonderland

10 Green Thumb Adventures

11 Artistic Explorers Club

Super Dresser Explorer

The Shoe Tango

In the morning, when the sun's aglow,
It's time to play the shoe tango!
Left foot, right foot, a dance so sweet,
Silly shoes upon my feet!
Jump and jive, it's a shoe parade,
Mixing up shoes, oh, what a charade!
Mismatched sneakers, a style divine,
In my shoe tango, every pair is mine!
So dance along, don't be shy,
The shoe tango is the way to fly.

The Adventure of Dressing Myself

Hello, little fashionistas! Have you ever dreamed of dressing yourself in the morning, choosing your favorite clothes and making your own style statement? Well, guess what? You can! In this exciting guide, we'll explore the world of independent dressing. Get ready for a journey full of fun, learning, and a few giggles along the way!
In my shoes, I'll never stop!

Dressing Like a Pro

Start Simple:

Let's kick off our dressing adventure with simple clothes. Choose comfy t-shirts, easy-to-pull-on pants, and sneakers or shoes with Velcro straps. No need to worry about tricky buttons and laces just yet.

Colorful Labels:

Make your clothes even more awesome by adding labels or pictures. Stick a colorful tag on your shirt or pants to know which is which. It's like giving your clothes secret identities!

Cool Routine:

Create a cool dressing routine. Make a chart with pictures or drawings to show the steps. Follow your chart every day, and soon you'll be dressing like a pro, all by yourself.

Dressing Like a Pro

Pick Your Style:

Want to be a superhero today or a princess tomorrow? You get to choose! Ask your grown-up to lay out a few outfits, and then pick the one that makes you feel fantastic. It's your chance to show off your style!

Dressing Tools:

Use some superhero tools to help you with tricky stuff. Zipper pulls and button hooks are like magic wands for dressing. They make zipping and buttoning super easy!

Happy Celebrations:

Every time you dress yourself, celebrate! Give yourself a high-five or do a little dance. You're becoming a dressing superhero, and that calls for a party!

The ABCs of Dressing Fun

Time Flies:

Sometimes dressing takes a bit longer when you're learning. Don't rush! Enjoy each step of the process, and soon you'll be as fast as a superhero changing into their costume.

Be Unique:

Your clothes, your way! Mix and match colors, wear socks with fun patterns, and create your own style. The more unique, the better!

Roll With It:

As you learn, you might face new challenges. Maybe a tricky zipper or a button that won't cooperate. No worries! Take a deep breath, and ask for help if you need it. You're still a dressing champion!

The ABCs of Dressing Fun

Weather Wizards:

Dressing isn't just about looking cool; it's about being comfy too. Learn about different clothes for different weather. Jackets for chilly days, shorts for sunny days – you're becoming a weather wizard!

Funny Moments:

Laugh along the way! Sometimes clothes can be silly, and that's okay. Ever put your shirt on backward or your shoes on the wrong feet? It happens to the best of us! Just giggle and fix it.

Mia's Marvelous Morning

Mia, has a passion for picking out her own clothes. One morning, Mia decided to dress herself from head to toe. She looked at her cool routine chart, chose a bright outfit with flowers and stripes, and even added a superhero cape!

As Mia put on her socks, she realized one had polka dots and the other had stripes. Instead of changing them, she laughed and said, "Mix and match is my style today!" Mia felt like a fashion superhero, ready to conquer the day with her unique look.

Mia's mom smiled, seeing her daughter's confidence grow. Mia skipped out the door, proud of her independent dressing skills. And so, Mia's marvelous morning became a story of dressing triumph and a whole lot of fun!

Manners Magic: The Power of Politeness

Knock, Knock!
Knock, knock!
Who's there?
Please.
Please who?
Please let me in; it's cold out here!

Saying "Please" and "Thank You"

Hello, little friends! Have you ever wondered about the magic words that make everyone smile? Well, those magical words are "Please" and "Thank You"! In this section, we'll dive into the world of politeness and learn how saying these words can create happiness and warmth around us.

Mastering the Magic Words

Start with a Smile:

Before you say anything, give your biggest, brightest smile. It's like opening a door to kindness!

"Please," The Magic Request:

When you want something, use the word "Please." Whether it's asking for a cookie or a turn on the swing, saying "Please" makes your request extra special.

"Thank You," The Gratitude Song:

When someone does something nice for you, sing the "Thank You" song! Say, "Thank You" with a big, happy heart. It shows that you appreciate their kindness.

Mastering the Magic Words

Practice, Practice, Practice:

Practice saying "Please" and "Thank You" every day. You can practice with your family, friends, or even your favorite teddy bear! The more you practice, the more magical it becomes.

Sharing is Caring:

Share your toys, snacks, or even a story with a friend. When they say "Please" and "Thank You," you'll feel like a friendship wizard, spreading kindness everywhere!

Magic Words Everywhere:

Use your magic words not only at home but also at school, the park, and anywhere you go. You'll see how these words create a trail of smiles wherever you are.

The Secrets of Politeness

Kindness Sparks:

Saying "Please" and "Thank You" is like sprinkling kindness sparks around you. It makes people feel happy and appreciated.

Sharing Sunshine:

When you share your magic words, you're like a little sunshine that brightens someone's day. It's a superpower of kindness!

Manners Matter:

Using good manners, like saying "Please" and "Thank You," is like having a secret code of politeness. It makes you stand out in the best way!

Friendship Flourishes:

Magic words create a garden of friendship. When you share them, you're planting seeds of kindness that grow into strong, happy friendships.

Happy Heart, Happy World:

Your heart feels happy when you say "Please" and "Thank You," and that happiness spreads to everyone around you. It's like a joy party!

The Thank You Adventure

Once upon a time, in a colorful town, lived a curious 6-year-old named Alex. One day, Alex's friend Lily shared her crayons for a drawing adventure. Excitedly, Alex said, "Thank You" with a big smile.

As days passed, Alex made a Thank You adventure game. Every time someone did something nice, Alex would say "Thank You" and draw a little star on a special Thank You card. The card became a magical treasure, filled with stars and gratitude.

One day, Alex decided to give the Thank You card to Lily. When Lily opened it, she saw the stars and felt like she had just found a secret map to happiness. From that day on, Alex and Lily continued their adventures, spreading kindness and collecting stars together.

Remember, my little friends, saying "Please" and "Thank You" is like using a sprinkle of kindness magic. It makes the world brighter, and you become a hero of politeness! So, let's spread the magic words and watch kindness bloom around us!

Sharing Stars

Sharing, sharing, here we go, In our hearts, the joy will grow. Take a turn, give a smile, Sharing makes our time worthwhile. Sharing, sharing, hand in hand, Spreading joy across the land. Friends together, happy and free, Sharing is the key.

The Joy of Sharing

Hello, dear friends! Have you ever experienced the warm fuzzies that come from sharing with your pals? Sharing is like sprinkling happiness around, and in this delightful section, we're going to explore the joy of sharing with our peers. Get ready for a journey of friendship, kindness, and lots of smiles!

Becoming a Sharing Superstar

Friendly Smile:

Start by wearing your friendliest smile. It's the magical key that opens the door to sharing joy.

Ask Nicely:

When you want to share, ask your friend nicely if they'd like to join in the fun. Say, "Would you like to play with this too?" or "Do you want to share snacks?"

Divide and Conquer:

If you have a toy or a snack, show your friend how you can divide it into two parts. Sharing means everyone gets a piece of the joy!

Turn-Taking Time:

If you're playing a game or using something special, take turns. Let your friend have a turn and then enjoy your turn. It's like dancing together in the sharing dance!

Sharing Space:

Sometimes sharing isn't just about things; it's about space too. If you're playing in a special spot, invite your friend to join in the adventure.

Celebrate Together:

When you and your friend share, celebrate! You can do a happy dance, clap your hands, or even sing a sharing song. The more you celebrate, the more joy you spread.

The ABCs of Sharing Fun

Double the Joy:

Sharing doubles the fun! When you share a game or a treat, you're creating joy not only for yourself but for your friend too. It's like having a joy party!

Friendship Blooms:

Sharing is like planting seeds of friendship. As you share, you watch your friendship garden bloom with colorful flowers of joy and kindness.

Kindness Ripples:

When you share, you create ripples of kindness that touch everyone around you. It's like throwing pebbles of joy into a pond and watching the happiness spread.

Teamwork Triumphs:

Sharing is teamwork! When you and your friend share, you're a superhero team creating a world of joy and laughter together.

Smiles Everywhere:

The more you share, the more smiles you see. It's like a treasure hunt for smiles, and you're the captain of the joy brigade!

The Magical Sharing Blanket

Once upon a time, in a sunny neighborhood, lived two friends named Tina and Sam. One day, Tina brought out her favorite magical blanket that could turn into anything they imagined.

Tina, with her friendly smile, said, "Sam, want to share the magical blanket adventure?" Sam's eyes sparkled, and with excitement, he said, "Yes, please!"

As they played together under the magical blanket, they took turns being pirates, explorers, and even astronauts. Each time they switched roles, they giggled and celebrated. The magical sharing blanket turned their ordinary day into an extraordinary adventure of joy and friendship.

Street Safety Safari

The Street-Crossing Shuffle

Left, right, left, and then, Do the street-crossing shuffle again. Hold a hand, don't run wild, Safety dance for every child. Green light, it's time to go, Cross the street nice and slow. Look for cars, listen too, The street-crossing shuffle, just for you! Turning left, turning right, Stay alert and hold on tight. Sidewalk boogie, one, two, three, Street-crossing fun for you and me!

Crossing the Street Safely

Hello, little adventurers! Have you ever wondered about the magical journey of crossing the street safely? Well, put on your safety hats and get ready for a fantastic exploration! In this section, we'll learn how to cross the street like safety superheroes, keeping our adventures safe and sound.

The Street-Crossing Adventure

Stop, Look, and Listen:

The first step in our adventure is to stop at the edge of the sidewalk. Take a moment to look left, right, and left again. Listen for any sounds of cars or bikes approaching.

Hold Hands:

If you're with a grown-up, hold their hand tightly. It's like having a safety sidekick on your street-crossing adventure. If you're alone, be extra careful and look out for your safety.

Find the Safe Spot:

Look for a crosswalk or a pedestrian crossing with stripes. This is your magical path to the other side. Head towards this safe spot as you continue your adventure.

The Street-Crossing Adventure

Green Means Go:

If there's a traffic light, wait for it to turn green. Green means it's time to go! If there's a walk sign, cross when it's lit up. Always follow the signals to stay safe on your journey.

One Step at a Time:

Walk, don't run, across the street. Take one step at a time and keep looking left and right as you move forward. It's like doing a safety dance!

Look Out for Turning Cars:

Even when the light is green, keep an eye out for cars turning. Some cars may be making a turn, so always be aware and stay on your toes.

Street-Crossing Wisdom

Stay on the Sidewalk:

The sidewalk is your safety zone. Always walk on the sidewalk, away from the edge, to avoid getting too close to the street.

Hold Hands with a Grown-Up:

If you're with a grown-up, holding hands is like having a safety shield. It shows drivers that you're with someone responsible, making your adventure even safer.

Use Crosswalks:

Crosswalks are like magical bridges for street-crossing adventures. Always use them when available, and follow the painted lines to guide your way.

Street-Crossing Wisdom

Traffic Signs are Friends:

Pay attention to traffic signs. They're like friendly guides giving you clues about when it's safe to cross or when you should wait.

Look Left, Right, and Left Again:

The street-crossing mantra is to look left, right, and left again. Make it a habit, and you'll be a street-crossing expert in no time.

Benny's Big Street Adventure

Meet Benny, a brave explorer who loved going on big street adventures with his dog, Sparky. One sunny day, Benny and Sparky decided to explore the park on the other side of the street.

Before starting their adventure, Benny remembered his safety rules. He stopped at the edge of the sidewalk, looked left, right, and left again. Benny held Sparky's leash tightly and found the crosswalk, their magical path to the other side.

As the traffic light turned green, Benny and Sparky took one step at a time, following the painted lines of the crosswalk. Benny made sure to keep an eye out for turning cars and listened for any sounds around.

Their adventure was a success! Benny and Sparky reached the park safely, ready to explore and play. Benny knew that following the safety rules made every street adventure a fun and secure experience.

Now, my little explorers, put on your adventure hats and remember these safety tips. Crossing the street safely is like embarking on a magical journey, and with your safety skills, every adventure will be full of joy and excitement!

Stranger Safety Squad

The Safety Shuffle

Stay with buddies, hold their hand, In safe spaces, let's make a stand. Say no to treats, gifts, or a ride, The safety shuffle, our safety pride. Use your super voice, loud and clear, If a stranger comes too near. Run to safety, fast as can be, The safety shuffle, it's you and me! Know your safe adults, make a plan, Trust your instincts, you're a safety fan.

Staying Safe and Sound: Stranger Danger Awareness

Hello, little heroes! Today, we're going to talk about a super important topic - staying safe from strangers. Our journey will be like becoming guardians of our safety! So, put on your safety capes, and let's learn all about stranger danger awareness.

Becoming Safety Superheroes

Stay with a Buddy:

Always have a buddy when you're playing outside or walking home. It's like having a superhero partner to keep each other safe.

Safe Spaces Only:

Stick to places you know are safe, like your home, school, or a friend's house. Avoid going to unfamiliar places without a grown-up you trust.

Staying Safe and Sound: Stranger Danger Awareness

Say No to Gifts or Treats:

If a stranger offers you gifts, treats, or toys, always say no. Real superheroes don't accept things from people they don't know.

Use Your Super Voice:

If a stranger tries to talk to you or make you feel uncomfortable, use your super voice. Yell, "NO!" or "HELP!" to let people around you know you need assistance.

Run to Safety:

If you ever feel scared or uneasy, run to a safe place. Find a trusted adult, like a teacher, police officer, or a mom with kids, and tell them what happened.

Know Your Safe Adults:

Make a list of safe adults – people you can trust. Share this list with your family, and make sure everyone knows who your safe adults are.

The ABCs of Stranger Danger

Strangers Can Be Tricky:

Not all strangers are bad, but it's essential to be cautious. If someone you don't know tries to take you somewhere or make you do something, it's time to be extra careful.

Trusted Adults Are Key:

Your family, teachers, and other grown-ups you know well are like your superhero squad. If you ever feel uneasy, go to them for help.

Secrets Aren't Safe:

Real superheroes don't keep secrets from their trusted adults. If someone tells you to keep something a secret, it's a red flag. Share it with a grown-up you trust.

The ABCs of Stranger Danger

Follow Your Instincts:

If something doesn't feel right, listen to your instincts. Your feelings are like a superhero power that keeps you safe. Trust them!

Safety Plan:

Talk to your family about what to do in different situations. Having a safety plan is like having a shield that protects you from potential danger.

Emma and the Safe Stranger Encounter

Once upon a time, in a cozy town, lived a brave 6-year-old named Emma. One day, as Emma was playing at the park, a friendly-looking stranger approached her. The stranger had a puppy and offered to let Emma pet it. Emma remembered her superhero training. She politely said, "No, thank you," and quickly ran to a safe spot where other kids were playing. Emma knew that even though the stranger seemed nice, it was essential to be cautious and stay with her friends.

When Emma reached the safe spot, she saw a mom with her children. Emma went up to the mom and told her about the encounter. The mom appreciated Emma's awareness and thanked her for being brave and smart. Emma felt proud of herself for handling the situation like a true safety superhero.

Now, my little safety superheroes, you've learned the ABCs of stranger danger awareness. Keep your safety capes on, and remember, being cautious doesn't mean being scared—it means being smart and strong! With your superhero knowledge, you're ready to face the world with confidence and stay safe and sound.

911 Explorers

Emergency, emergency, call for help so free, Dial the numbers on the phone, superheroes come to me. Police, fire, medical, too, Help is on the way for you. Emergency, emergency, call for help so free, Dial the numbers, you will see.

Heroes on Speed Dial: Emergency Phone Numbers

Greetings, little heroes! Today, we're going to talk about something very special - emergency phone numbers. Imagine having a secret code that can bring superheroes to your rescue! In this section, we'll discover the magic of emergency phone numbers and how they turn ordinary moments into superhero adventures.

Dialing for Heroes - The Emergency Phone Number Adventure

Know Your Numbers:

Memorize the important emergency phone numbers. For most places, it's 911. This number is like a superhero hotline, connecting you to help when you need it most.

Find a Phone:

If you ever find yourself in an emergency, look for a phone nearby. It can be a cell phone or a landline. Knowing where to find a phone is like having a treasure map to safety.

Stay Calm:

In case of an emergency, take a deep breath and stay calm. Superheroes think clearly even in tough situations. You've got this!

Dial the Numbers:

Pick up the phone and dial the emergency number. If it's 911, say it loud and clear. Remember, the superheroes on the other end are ready to help you.

Talk Clearly:

When the operator answers, talk clearly and tell them what's happening. Share your name, where you are, and what kind of help you need. Superheroes rely on clear communication!

Follow Instructions:

Listen carefully to the instructions given by the operator. They are like superhero guides, helping you stay safe until help arrives.

The Superpower of Emergency Numbers

Help is a Call Away:

Emergency phone numbers are like magical calls that summon help. Whether it's firefighters, police, or medical assistance, these numbers connect you to heroes in a flash.

Practice Makes Perfect:

Practice dialing emergency numbers with your family. It's like training for a superhero mission. The more you practice, the more confident you become.

Know Your Address:

In emergencies, knowing your address is crucial. It's like giving superheroes a roadmap to find you quickly. Practice saying your address out loud with your family.

Tell a Grown-Up:

Make sure a grown-up you trust knows the emergency numbers too. It's like having a superhero ally who can help you in case you need to make the call.

Don't Be Afraid:

Emergency numbers are there to help, not to scare you. Knowing them is like having a shield that keeps you safe. Remember, heroes are on their way!

Sarah's Super Call

Once upon a time in a friendly neighborhood, lived a superhero named Sarah. One day, Sarah and her little brother were playing in the park when they noticed someone who needed help. Sarah remembered her superhero training and knew it was time to make the super call.

With a calm heart, Sarah found a phone booth nearby. She dialed 911 and spoke to the operator. She shared her name, the park's address, and explained the situation. The operator was like a superhero guide, giving Sarah instructions until the real-life heroes arrived.

Sarah's super call brought firefighters to rescue a kitten stuck in a tree. The firefighters thanked Sarah for being a brave superhero and using the emergency number wisely. From that day on, Sarah felt even more powerful, knowing that she had a superhero hotline at her fingertips.

Now, little heroes, you've unlocked the secret of emergency phone numbers. Keep them in your superhero toolkit, practice with your family, and remember, heroes are just a call away. With your superpower knowledge, you're ready to face any adventure and keep yourself and others safe!

Coin Counting Quest

Ahoy, young treasure hunters! Today, we embark on a thrilling adventure into the world of counting money. Imagine turning shiny coins into magical treasures! In this section, we'll learn the art of counting coins, discovering the excitement and joy that comes with unlocking the secrets of currency.

Counting Coins - The Treasure Hunt Adventure

Meet the Coins:

Get to know the coins in your treasure chest - pennies, nickels, dimes, and quarters. Each coin has a unique value, and together, they create a treasure trove.

Understand Coin Values:

Learn the values of each coin. A penny is worth 1 cent, a nickel is worth 5 cents, a dime is worth 10 cents, and a quarter is worth 25 cents. It's like decoding the secret language of treasure hunters.

Start with Pennies:

Begin your counting adventure with pennies. Arrange them in stacks of 1, and count by ones. For example, if you have five pennies, you have 5 cents.

Add Nickels:

Introduce nickels to your treasure chest. Count them in groups of 5, as each nickel is worth 5 cents. For instance, if you have two nickels, you have 10 cents.

Include Dimes:

Level up your counting skills with dimes. Count them in groups of 10, as each dime is worth 10 cents. If you have three dimes, you have 30 cents.

Bring in the Quarters:

Elevate your counting adventure by adding quarters. Count them in groups of 25, as each quarter is worth 25 cents. If you have four quarters, you have 100 cents or $1.

The Riches of Counting Coins

Adding Up the Riches:

Combining different coins allows you to count larger amounts. For example, if you have three quarters (75 cents) and two dimes (20 cents), you add them together to get 95 cents.

Trade and Exchange:

Discover the art of trading coins. Trade five pennies for a nickel, and trade two nickels for a dime. It's like being a clever merchant in the treasure market.

Make Change:

Imagine buying a small treasure with your coins. If the treasure costs 15 cents and you pay with a quarter, you get change back. Learn to count the change you receive.

Saving for Bigger Treasures:

Counting coins can help you save for bigger treasures. Create a piggy bank or a treasure chest, and watch your savings grow.

Lily's Lemonade Stand Adventure

Once upon a sunny day, Lily, decided to open a lemonade stand in her neighborhood. She set up a small table with a sign that read, "Lily's Lemonade - 25 cents per cup."

As customers approached, Lily greeted them with a smile. When someone handed her a quarter, Lily knew they had paid the exact amount for a cup of lemonade. If a customer gave her three dimes, Lily counted by tens to make sure they had paid 30 cents.

As the day went on, Lily encountered different combinations of coins. Some customers paid with nickels and pennies, while others used quarters and dimes. Lily became a master of counting coins, making sure every customer received the correct change.

At the end of the day, Lily counted her earnings and realized she had collected a variety of coins. She felt proud of her counting skills and the success of her lemonade stand adventure.

Congratulations, young treasure hunters! You've mastered the art of counting coins, turning everyday moments into exciting adventures. Whether you're running a lemonade stand or saving for a special treasure, counting coins is a skill that opens the door to a world of possibilities. So, keep counting, keep exploring, and may your treasure chests be forever filled with shiny coins!

Table Setting Time Wizards

Hello, little magicians of the dining realm! Today, we embark on an enchanting journey into the art of setting and clearing the table. Picture turning an ordinary meal time into a grand feast! In this section, we'll unravel the secrets of table-setting magic and the joy of clearing the way for the next culinary adventure.

The Table-Setting and Clearing Spell

Gather Your Tools:
Prepare for your magical feast by gathering the tools of the trade - plates, forks, knives, spoons, napkins, and maybe even a sprinkle of fairy dust for extra charm.

The Plate Ballet:
Begin the dance of setting the table by placing a plate in front of each chair. It's like arranging seats for the honored guests in your magical kingdom.

Summon the Silverware Soldiers:
Introduce the silverware soldiers - forks, knives, and spoons. Place them in their designated spots, like soldiers standing tall in formation. The fork goes to the left, and the knife and spoon to the right.

Napkin Elegance:

Fold the napkins with care and place them beside the plate or artfully arrange them on top. Napkins are like the capes for your magical utensils, adding a touch of elegance to the feast.

Goblets and Chalices:

If you have magical goblets or chalices, position them above the knives and spoons. These vessels are ready to hold the most enchanted potions and elixirs.

Finishing Touches:

Add any finishing touches, like place cards or decorative elements. It's the extra sparkle that makes your magical feast truly extraordinary.

The Feast Begins:

Once the table is set, it's time for the grand feast to commence. Gather around with your fellow wizards and magical creatures to enjoy the enchanting spread.

Clearing the Way:

As the feast concludes, embark on the clearing spell. Gather the used plates, utensils, and napkins, and clear the way for the next mystical culinary adventure.

The Magic of Table Manners

Respect the Table Kingdom:

Treating the table with respect is like honoring the magical kingdom where feasts unfold. Keep the table neat and tidy for a dining experience fit for royalty.

Teamwork Makes Magic Work:

Enlist the help of your fellow wizards and magical creatures. Setting and clearing the table is a magical team effort that turns ordinary meals into extraordinary banquets.

The Art of Clearing:

Clearing the table is like creating a blank canvas for the next culinary masterpiece. Embrace the art of clearing, and the table will be ready to host new enchantments.

Reuse and Recreate:

Don't forget the magic of recycling. Clearing the table involves sorting items for reuse or recycling, contributing to the well-being of your magical kingdom and the real world.

The Feast of Whimsical Wonders

In a magical land where dragons soared and fairies fluttered, lived a young wizard named Oliver. One day, Oliver decided to host a feast of whimsical wonders for his friends in the enchanted forest.

With a wave of his wand, Oliver set the table with mystical plates, silverware, and goblets that sparkled like stars. Each seat had a personalized place card, creating an atmosphere of enchantment. As the feast unfolded, magical creatures from the enchanted forest joined the celebration. There were elves, unicorns, and even a mischievous pixie or two. The table setting added a touch of magic to the meal, turning it into a feast fit for kings and queens.

Once the last sip of enchanted nectar was taken and the final crumb of fairy bread vanished, Oliver and his friends embarked on the clearing spell. With laughter and camaraderie, they cleared the table, leaving the space ready for the next mystical banquet.

Congratulations, little magicians! You've now mastered the art of setting and clearing the table, transforming mealtime into a magical adventure. With your newfound skills, every feast becomes an enchanting experience, filled with whimsical wonders and the joy of shared meals. So, wave your wands, set your tables, and let the magical feasts continue in your enchanted realm!

Litter-Free Wonderland

Oh, listen up, my friends so dear, Captain Clean's message you'll want to hear. Say "no" to litter, let's make a stand, Protect our planet, it's Team Earth's command.

The Adventures of Captain Clean: Defending Our Planet from Litter

Ahoy, little eco-warriors! Today, we embark on an exciting journey alongside Captain Clean to discover the magical world of not littering. Imagine becoming guardians of our planet, keeping it sparkling and beautiful! In this section, we'll learn the art of saying "no" to litter and "yes" to a cleaner, greener Earth.

Captain Clean's Anti-Littering Superpowers

The Litter Shield:

Imagine you have a magical shield, just like Captain Clean! Use it to protect our planet from the evil forces of litter. Say "no" to dropping trash on the ground.

The Recycling Spell:

Learn the recycling spell to transform your trash into treasure. Keep a separate bag for recyclables like paper, plastic, and cans. Captain Clean knows that recycling is like turning old things into new adventures.

Pocket Pals:

Equip yourself with pocket pals—small bags or containers—to collect your trash. Captain Clean always keeps his pocket pals handy to capture any stray wrappers or bits of paper.

The Super Sweep:

If you see litter around, channel your inner superhero with the super sweep! Use a broom, your hands, or even a stick to gather the litter and dispose of it properly.

Trash Bin Tag Team:

Join forces with the trash bins in your neighborhood. Play a game of bin tag, where you try to tag the bin with your trash from a distance. It's a fun way to make sure every piece of litter finds its home.

The Litter-Free Code of Honor

Nature's Home:

Understand that our planet is the home of magical creatures, from soaring birds to tiny bugs. Littering disrupts their homes and can harm them. Captain Clean knows that every creature deserves a clean and safe habitat.

Team Earth:

Remember that we're all part of Team Earth. When you litter, it's like scoring a goal against your own team. Captain Clean believes that by keeping our planet clean, we're ensuring victory for Team Earth!

The Three Rs:

Captain Clean follows the three Rs—Reduce, Reuse, Recycle. Reduce the amount of trash you create, reuse items whenever possible, and recycle to give things a new life. It's the superhero way to protect the environment.

Trash Detective:

Become a trash detective like Captain Clean. Spot litterbugs and kindly remind them to use their anti-litter superpowers. Together, we can create a league of litter-free superheroes.

Captain Clean's Great Cleanup Quest

Once upon a time, in a land not too far away, lived Captain Clean, the mightiest superhero in the Litter-Free Kingdom. One day, Captain Clean noticed that litterbugs were trying to invade the kingdom and spread their trashy chaos.

With a twirl of his cape, Captain Clean activated his anti-littering superpowers. He equipped himself with the Litter Shield, the Recycling Spell, and his trusty Pocket Pals. Captain Clean zoomed through the kingdom, picking up litter and educating the residents about the importance of keeping their home clean.

As Captain Clean ventured into the enchanted forest, he encountered a mischievous litterbug named Larry the Litterbug. Larry was about to toss a candy wrapper on the ground when Captain Clean swooped in with his super sweep. He showed Larry the magical ways of pocket pals and the recycling spell, transforming Larry into a reformed litter-fighter.

The Litter-Free Kingdom sparkled once again, thanks to Captain Clean's Great Cleanup Quest. Residents and creatures alike joined Captain Clean's team, vowing to protect their magical home from the clutches of litter.

Hooray, little eco-warriors! You've now joined the ranks of Captain Clean in the quest to keep our planet litter-free. With your anti-litter superpowers, the Litter-Free Kingdom will remain a magical haven for all its inhabitants. So, remember the code, wield your shield, and let's continue our journey as guardians of this beautiful Earth!

Green Thumb Adventures

Hello, little garden guardians! Today, we embark on a magical journey into the world of plants and the art of taking care of them. Imagine becoming the keepers of a secret garden, where flowers bloom, and leaves twirl with joy! In this section, we'll explore the wonders of plant care, learning how to keep our leafy friends happy and healthy.

The Garden Guardian's Guide to Plant Care

The Watering Wand:
Imagine you have a magical watering wand, like the ones used by garden guardians. Hold it gently and sprinkle water around the base of your plants. Be sure to give each plant just the right amount of water, like a refreshing drink on a hot day.

The Sun Dance:
Every plant loves a good sun dance. Find a sunny spot for your leafy friends to bask in the sunlight. It's like a warm hug that helps them grow strong and tall. Be sure not to leave them out in the scorching sun for too long!

The Soil Snuggle:

Plants need a cozy bed of soil to snuggle into. Make sure their soil is fluffy and not too hard. You can give them a gentle pat to let them know you care. Think of it like tucking your plants in for a good night's sleep.

The Leafy Language:

Plants have a special language, and they talk to us through their leaves. If the leaves look sad and droopy, it might mean they need a sip of water. If they're turning yellow, they might be getting too much water. Listen to the leafy language, and you'll become a plant whisperer!

The Petal Patrol:

Keep an eye out for any unwanted guests on your plant's petals. Sometimes, tiny insects might visit, and that's okay. You can gently shoo them away or ask a grown-up for help. It's like having your own petal patrol!

The Secrets of Plant Magic

Plants Are Living Beings:

Plants are like magical beings that can grow, breathe, and even talk in their own leafy language. Treat them with kindness, and they'll share their magic with you.

Water Wisely:

Not all plants like the same amount of water. Some like it wetter, while others prefer drier soil. Discover the watering needs of each of your leafy friends to keep them happy.

Sunshine Power:

Just like you feel energized in the sunshine, plants need sunlight to make their food. Choose sunny spots for your plants, but be mindful not to leave them in the sun for too long without a break.

Be Patient, Little Gardener:

Plants grow at their own pace, just like you. Be patient and watch as your leafy friends unfurl their magical petals and leaves. It's like witnessing a real-life fairy tale!

The Enchanted Bloom

In a little town nestled between rolling hills and babbling brooks, lived a curious 6-year-old named Lily. One day, Lily discovered a mysterious seed in her grandmother's garden. With sparkling eyes, she decided to plant it and see what magic it held.

Lily named the seed Sprout, and with her magical watering wand, she gave it a gentle sip. Sprout's tiny leaves began to unfurl, and a tiny stem pushed through the soil. Lily did the sun dance, ensuring Sprout basked in the golden rays.

As days turned into weeks, Lily noticed Sprout's leaves speaking to her. They wiggled and danced, telling Lily they were happy with the sun and water. Lily listened to the leafy language and adjusted her care accordingly.

One day, as the sun dipped low in the sky, Sprout surprised Lily with a burst of color. The tiny seed had transformed into a beautiful flower, its petals painted in hues of pink and purple. Lily felt like a true garden guardian, caring for a magical bloom that whispered secrets of nature.

Congratulations, little garden guardians! You've now embarked on the magical journey of taking care of plants. With your watering wands and leafy language skills, you'll watch your leafy friends grow into enchanted blooms. So, dance in the sunlight, listen to the whispers of the leaves, and continue your journey as keepers of the magical gardens around you!

Artistic Explorers Club

Hello, little artists! Today, we are diving into the colorful world of drawing and coloring, where imagination knows no bounds. Imagine creating your own magical realms and bringing characters to life! In this section, we'll explore the wonders of drawing and coloring, learning how to turn blank pages into vibrant masterpieces.

The Magic of Drawing and Coloring

The Mighty Pencil:

Imagine your pencil is a magic wand, ready to create anything you can dream of. Hold it gently and let your imagination flow. You can draw straight lines, curvy lines, or even zigzags. The pencil is your trusty sidekick in the world of art.

The Rainbow Palette:

Dive into the rainbow palette of colors. Choose your favorites and let them dance on the page. Reds, blues, greens, and yellows - the possibilities are endless. Each color is like a friend waiting to join your artistic adventure.

The Coloring Dance:

As you color, imagine a dance between your pencil and the paper. Stay inside the lines or let the colors flow freely. It's your dance, and there are no wrong moves. Coloring is a celebration of your creativity.

Add Details and Patterns:

Spice up your drawings with details and patterns. Dots, stripes, swirls - let your pencil dance across the page, creating textures and adding depth. Your drawings will come alive with every stroke.

Bring Characters to Life:

Turn your drawings into characters with personalities. Draw funny faces, give them clothes, or imagine them in exciting adventures. Your drawings can tell stories without a single word.

The Artistic Secrets

Art Is for Everyone:

Remember that art is for everyone, and there are no rules. Whether you're drawing stick figures or intricate scenes, it's your unique expression. Let your creativity flow, and don't be afraid to experiment.

The Joy of Mistakes:

Mistakes are like magical portals to new ideas. If your line wiggles or your colors mix unexpectedly, embrace the joy of mistakes. They often lead to happy surprises in your artwork.

Sharing Your Masterpieces:

Share your masterpieces with friends and family. Display them proudly on the fridge or create a mini art gallery in your room. Art is meant to be celebrated and shared.

Drawing Every Day:

Like any magical skill, drawing gets better with practice. Set aside a little time each day to doodle and draw. Soon, you'll see your artistic powers growing.

The Tale of Artists Past and Present

Throughout history, artists have used drawing and coloring as tools of expression. From ancient cave paintings to the masterpieces of Leonardo da Vinci and Vincent van Gogh, the art of drawing has evolved and captivated hearts.

Today, artists like Frida Kahlo, Banksy, and many others continue to inspire us with their unique styles and stories. Drawing and coloring have been bridges connecting people across time, cultures, and ages.

Congratulations, little artists! You've now unlocked the magical secrets of drawing and coloring. With your mighty pencils and rainbow palettes, you can turn any blank page into a canvas of wonder. So, let your creativity flow, dance with your pencil, and continue your journey as the magical artists you are. The world is your canvas, waiting to be filled with your unique creations!

www.ingramcontent.com/pod-product-compliance
Lightning Source LLC
Chambersburg PA
CBHW042120100526
44587CB00025B/4128